# My TravelJournal

---

DATE:            PLACE:

## HOW I FELT TODAY:

## WHAT I'VE SEEN TODAY:

_____
_____
_____
_____
_____
_____
_____
_____
_____
_____
_____
_____

## WHAT I ATE TODAY:

_____
_____
_____
_____
_____

## HOW DID WE TRAVEL:

## THE BEST THING THAT HAPPENED TOODAY:

_____
_____

## THE WEATHER TODAY WAS:

PLACE FOR DRAWINGS, PAINTINGS, WRITING, ENTRY TICKETS, PICTURES OR ALL THE OTHER STUFF YOU WANT TO CAPTURE

DATE: _____  PLACE: _____

## HOW I FELT TODAY:

## WHAT I'VE SEEN TODAY:

_____
_____
_____
_____
_____
_____
_____
_____
_____
_____
_____
_____

## WHAT I ATE TODAY:

_____
_____
_____
_____

### HOW DID WE TRAVEL:

## THE BEST THING THAT HAPPENED TOODAY:

_____
_____

## THE WEATHER TODAY WAS:

PLACE FOR DRAWINGS, PAINTINGS, WRITING, ENTRY TICKETS, PICTURES OR ALL THE OTHER STUFF YOU WANT TO CAPTURE

DATE:             PLACE:

## HOW I FELT TODAY:

| WHAT I'VE SEEN TODAY: | WHAT I ATE TODAY: |
|---|---|
| _____ | _____ |
| _____ | _____ |
| _____ | _____ |
| _____ | _____ |
| _____ | _____ |
| _____ | HOW DID WE TRAVEL: |
| _____ | |
| _____ | |
| _____ | |
| _____ | |
| _____ | |

## THE BEST THING THAT HAPPENED TOODAY:
_____
_____

## THE WEATHER TODAY WAS:

PLACE FOR DRAWINGS, PAINTINGS, WRITING, ENTRY TICKETS, PICTURES OR ALL THE OTHER STUFF YOU WANT TO CAPTURE

DATE: _____   PLACE: _____

HOW I FELT TODAY:

WHAT I'VE SEEN TODAY:

_____
_____
_____
_____
_____
_____
_____
_____
_____
_____
_____
_____

WHAT I ATE TODAY:

_____
_____
_____
_____

HOW DID WE TRAVEL:

THE BEST THING THAT HAPPENED TOODAY:

_____
_____

THE WEATHER TODAY WAS:

PLACE FOR DRAWINGS, PAINTINGS, WRITING, ENTRY TICKETS, PICTURES OR ALL THE OTHER STUFF YOU WANT TO CAPTURE

DATE: _____  PLACE: _____

## HOW I FELT TODAY:

## WHAT I'VE SEEN TODAY:

_____
_____
_____
_____
_____
_____
_____
_____
_____
_____
_____

## WHAT I ATE TODAY:

_____
_____
_____
_____

### HOW DID WE TRAVEL:

## THE BEST THING THAT HAPPENED TOODAY:

_____
_____

## THE WEATHER TODAY WAS:

PLACE FOR DRAWINGS, PAINTINGS, WRITING, ENTRY TICKETS, PICTURES OR ALL THE OTHER STUFF YOU WANT TO CAPTURE

DATE: _____  PLACE: _____

## HOW I FELT TODAY:

| WHAT I'VE SEEN TODAY: | WHAT I ATE TODAY: |
|---|---|
| _____ | _____ |
| _____ | _____ |
| _____ | _____ |
| _____ | _____ |
| _____ | _____ |
| _____ | **HOW DID WE TRAVEL:** |
| _____ | |
| _____ | |
| _____ | |
| _____ | |

## THE BEST THING THAT HAPPENED TOODAY:
_____
_____

## THE WEATHER TODAY WAS:

PLACE FOR DRAWINGS, PAINTINGS, WRITING, ENTRY TICKETS, PICTURES OR ALL THE OTHER STUFF YOU WANT TO CAPTURE

Date: ................................ Place: ................................

## How I felt Today:

| What I've Seen today: | What I Ate Today: |
| --- | --- |
| _____ | _____ |
| _____ | _____ |
| _____ | _____ |
| _____ | _____ |
| _____ | **How did we Travel:** |
| _____ | |
| _____ | |
| _____ | |
| _____ | |

## The Best Thing that happened tooday:
_____
_____

## The Weather today was:

PLACE FOR DRAWINGS, PAINTINGS, WRITING, ENTRY TICKETS, PICTURES OR ALL THE OTHER STUFF YOU WANT TO CAPTURE

DATE:          PLACE:

## HOW I FELT TODAY:

## WHAT I'VE SEEN TODAY:

_____
_____
_____
_____
_____
_____
_____
_____
_____
_____
_____

## WHAT I ATE TODAY:

_____
_____
_____
_____

### HOW DID WE TRAVEL:

## THE BEST THING THAT HAPPENED TOODAY:

_____
_____

## THE WEATHER TODAY WAS:

PLACE FOR DRAWINGS, PAINTINGS, WRITING, ENTRY TICKETS, PICTURES OR ALL THE OTHER STUFF YOU WANT TO CAPTURE

DATE: _____   PLACE: _____

HOW I FELT TODAY:

WHAT I'VE SEEN TODAY:

_____
_____
_____
_____
_____
_____
_____
_____
_____
_____

WHAT I ATE TODAY:

_____
_____
_____
_____

HOW DID WE TRAVEL:

THE BEST THING THAT HAPPENED TOODAY:

_____
_____

THE WEATHER TODAY WAS:

PLACE FOR DRAWINGS, PAINTINGS, WRITING, ENTRY TICKETS, PICTURES OR ALL THE OTHER STUFF YOU WANT TO CAPTURE

DATE: _____ PLACE: _____

HOW I FELT TODAY:

WHAT I'VE SEEN TODAY:

_____
_____
_____
_____
_____
_____
_____
_____
_____
_____
_____
_____

WHAT I ATE TODAY:

_____
_____
_____
_____

HOW DID WE TRAVEL:

THE BEST THING THAT HAPPENED TOODAY:

_____
_____

THE WEATHER TODAY WAS:

PLACE FOR DRAWINGS, PAINTINGS, WRITING, ENTRY TICKETS, PICTURES OR ALL THE OTHER STUFF YOU WANT TO CAPTURE

DATE:        PLACE:

## HOW I FELT TODAY:

## WHAT I'VE SEEN TODAY:

_____
_____
_____
_____
_____
_____
_____
_____
_____
_____
_____

## WHAT I ATE TODAY:

_____
_____
_____
_____

## HOW DID WE TRAVEL:

## THE BEST THING THAT HAPPENED TOODAY:
_____
_____

## THE WEATHER TODAY WAS:

PLACE FOR DRAWINGS, PAINTINGS, WRITING, ENTRY TICKETS, PICTURES OR ALL THE OTHER STUFF YOU WANT TO CAPTURE

DATE:                 PLACE:

## HOW I FELT TODAY:

## WHAT I'VE SEEN TODAY:

_____
_____
_____
_____
_____
_____
_____
_____
_____
_____
_____

## WHAT I ATE TODAY:

_____
_____
_____
_____

## HOW DID WE TRAVEL:

## THE BEST THING THAT HAPPENED TOODAY:

_____
_____

## THE WEATHER TODAY WAS:

PLACE FOR DRAWINGS, PAINTINGS, WRITING, ENTRY TICKETS, PICTURES OR ALL THE OTHER STUFF YOU WANT TO CAPTURE

Date: ................................. Place: .................................

How I felt Today:

| What I've Seen today: | What I Ate Today: |
|---|---|
| _____ | _____ |
| _____ | _____ |
| _____ | _____ |
| _____ | _____ |
| _____ | _____ |
| _____ | **How did we Travel:** |
| _____ | |
| _____ | |
| _____ | |
| _____ | |

The Best Thing that happened tooday:
_____
_____

The Weather today was:

PLACE FOR DRAWINGS, PAINTINGS, WRITING, ENTRY TICKETS, PICTURES OR ALL THE OTHER STUFF YOU WANT TO CAPTURE

DATE: .......................... PLACE: ..........................

HOW I FELT TODAY:

WHAT I'VE SEEN TODAY:

_____
_____
_____
_____
_____
_____
_____
_____
_____
_____
_____
_____

WHAT I ATE TODAY:

_____
_____
_____
_____

HOW DID WE TRAVEL:

THE BEST THING THAT HAPPENED TOODAY:

_____
_____

THE WEATHER TODAY WAS:

PLACE FOR DRAWINGS, PAINTINGS, WRITING, ENTRY TICKETS, PICTURES OR ALL THE OTHER STUFF YOU WANT TO CAPTURE

DATE:           PLACE:

## HOW I FELT TODAY:

## WHAT I'VE SEEN TODAY:

_____
_____
_____
_____
_____
_____
_____
_____
_____
_____

## WHAT I ATE TODAY:

_____
_____
_____
_____

### HOW DID WE TRAVEL:

## THE BEST THING THAT HAPPENED TOODAY:

_____
_____

## THE WEATHER TODAY WAS:

PLACE FOR DRAWINGS, PAINTINGS, WRITING, ENTRY TICKETS, PICTURES OR ALL THE OTHER STUFF YOU WANT TO CAPTURE

DATE: _____     PLACE: _____

HOW I FELT TODAY:

WHAT I'VE SEEN TODAY:

_____
_____
_____
_____
_____
_____
_____
_____
_____
_____
_____
_____
_____

WHAT I ATE TODAY:

_____
_____
_____
_____
_____

HOW DID WE TRAVEL:

THE BEST THING THAT HAPPENED TOODAY:
_____
_____

THE WEATHER TODAY WAS:

PLACE FOR DRAWINGS, PAINTINGS, WRITING, ENTRY TICKETS, PICTURES OR ALL THE OTHER STUFF YOU WANT TO CAPTURE

Date: _____     Place: _____

## How I felt Today:

| What I've Seen today: | What I Ate Today: |
|---|---|
| _____ | _____ |
| _____ | _____ |
| _____ | _____ |
| _____ | _____ |
| _____ | _____ |
| _____ | **How did we Travel:** |
| _____ | |
| _____ | |
| _____ | |
| _____ | |

## The Best Thing that happened tooday:
_____
_____

## The Weather today was:

PLACE FOR DRAWINGS, PAINTINGS, WRITING, ENTRY TICKETS, PICTURES OR ALL THE OTHER STUFF YOU WANT TO CAPTURE

DATE:      PLACE:

HOW I FELT TODAY:

WHAT I'VE SEEN TODAY:

_____
_____
_____
_____
_____
_____
_____
_____
_____
_____
_____

WHAT I ATE TODAY:

_____
_____
_____
_____
_____

HOW DID WE TRAVEL:

THE BEST THING THAT HAPPENED TOODAY:

_____
_____

THE WEATHER TODAY WAS:

PLACE FOR DRAWINGS, PAINTINGS, WRITING, ENTRY TICKETS, PICTURES OR ALL THE OTHER STUFF YOU WANT TO CAPTURE

Date:          Place:

## How I felt Today:

## What I've Seen today:

_____
_____
_____
_____
_____
_____
_____
_____
_____
_____
_____

## What I Ate Today:

_____
_____
_____
_____
_____

## How did we Travel:

## The Best Thing that happened tooday:

_____
_____

## The Weather today was:

PLACE FOR DRAWINGS, PAINTINGS, WRITING, ENTRY TICKETS, PICTURES OR ALL THE OTHER STUFF YOU WANT TO CAPTURE

DATE:           PLACE:

## HOW I FELT TODAY:

## WHAT I'VE SEEN TODAY:

_____
_____
_____
_____
_____
_____
_____
_____
_____
_____
_____
_____

## WHAT I ATE TODAY:

_____
_____
_____
_____
_____

### HOW DID WE TRAVEL:

## THE BEST THING THAT HAPPENED TOODAY:

_____
_____

## THE WEATHER TODAY WAS:

PLACE FOR DRAWINGS, PAINTINGS, WRITING, ENTRY TICKETS, PICTURES OR ALL THE OTHER STUFF YOU WANT TO CAPTURE

Date: _____ | Place: _____

## How I felt Today:

| What I've Seen today: | What I Ate Today: |
|---|---|
| _____ | _____ |
| _____ | _____ |
| _____ | _____ |
| _____ | _____ |
| _____ | _____ |
| _____ | **How did we Travel:** |
| _____ | |
| _____ | |
| _____ | |
| _____ | |

## The Best Thing that happened tooday:

_____

_____

## The Weather today was:

PLACE FOR DRAWINGS, PAINTINGS, WRITING, ENTRY TICKETS, PICTURES OR ALL THE OTHER STUFF YOU WANT TO CAPTURE

Date: _____  Place: _____

How I felt Today:

What I've Seen today:
_____
_____
_____
_____
_____
_____
_____
_____
_____
_____
_____
_____

What I Ate Today:
_____
_____
_____
_____

How did we Travel:

The Best Thing that happened tooday:
_____
_____

The Weather today was:

PLACE FOR DRAWINGS, PAINTINGS, WRITING, ENTRY TICKETS, PICTURES OR ALL THE OTHER STUFF YOU WANT TO CAPTURE

DATE: _____  PLACE: _____

## HOW I FELT TODAY:

## WHAT I'VE SEEN TODAY:

_____
_____
_____
_____
_____
_____
_____
_____
_____
_____
_____

## WHAT I ATE TODAY:

_____
_____
_____
_____

## HOW DID WE TRAVEL:

## THE BEST THING THAT HAPPENED TOODAY:
_____
_____

## THE WEATHER TODAY WAS:

PLACE FOR DRAWINGS, PAINTINGS, WRITING, ENTRY TICKETS, PICTURES OR ALL THE OTHER STUFF YOU WANT TO CAPTURE

DATE:      PLACE:

HOW I FELT TODAY:

WHAT I'VE SEEN TODAY:

_____
_____
_____
_____
_____
_____
_____
_____
_____
_____

WHAT I ATE TODAY:

_____
_____
_____
_____

HOW DID WE TRAVEL:

THE BEST THING THAT HAPPENED TOODAY:

_____
_____

THE WEATHER TODAY WAS:

PLACE FOR DRAWINGS, PAINTINGS, WRITING, ENTRY TICKETS, PICTURES OR ALL THE OTHER STUFF YOU WANT TO CAPTURE

DATE: PLACE:

HOW I FELT TODAY:

WHAT I'VE SEEN TODAY:

_____
_____
_____
_____
_____
_____
_____
_____
_____
_____
_____
_____

WHAT I ATE TODAY:

_____
_____
_____
_____

HOW DID WE TRAVEL:

THE BEST THING THAT HAPPENED TOODAY:
_____
_____

THE WEATHER TODAY WAS:

PLACE FOR DRAWINGS, PAINTINGS, WRITING, ENTRY TICKETS, PICTURES OR ALL THE OTHER STUFF YOU WANT TO CAPTURE

Date: _____ Place: _____

How I felt Today:

😃 🙂 😐 😍 😎 😫

What I've Seen today: _____ What I Ate Today:
_____ _____
_____ _____
_____ _____
_____ _____
_____ _____
_____
_____ How did we Travel:
_____
_____
_____
_____
_____

The Best Thing that happened tooday:
_____
_____

THE Weather today was:

☀️ ☁️ ⛈️ 🌧️ 🌨️

PLACE FOR DRAWINGS, PAINTINGS, WRITING, ENTRY TICKETS, PICTURES OR ALL THE OTHER STUFF YOU WANT TO CAPTURE

DATE: _____  PLACE: _____

## HOW I FELT TODAY:

😀 🙂 😐 😍 😎 😫

| WHAT I'VE SEEN TODAY: | WHAT I ATE TODAY: |
|---|---|
| _____ | _____ |
| _____ | _____ |
| _____ | _____ |
| _____ | _____ |
| _____ | _____ |
| _____ | **HOW DID WE TRAVEL:** |
| _____ | |
| _____ | |
| _____ | |
| _____ | |

## THE BEST THING THAT HAPPENED TOODAY:

_____

_____

## THE WEATHER TODAY WAS:

☀️ ☁️ ⛈️ 🌧️ 🌨️

PLACE FOR DRAWINGS, PAINTINGS, WRITING, ENTRY TICKETS, PICTURES OR ALL THE OTHER STUFF YOU WANT TO CAPTURE

DATE: _____    PLACE: _____

## How I felt Today:

😃  🙂  😐  😍  😎  😩

## What I've Seen today:

_____
_____
_____
_____
_____
_____
_____
_____
_____
_____
_____

## What I Ate Today:

_____
_____
_____
_____

## How did we Travel:

🚂  ✈️
🚗  🚢

## The Best Thing that happened tooday:

_____
_____

## The Weather today was:

☀️  ☁️  ⛈️  🌧️  🌨️

PLACE FOR DRAWINGS, PAINTINGS, WRITING, ENTRY TICKETS, PICTURES OR ALL THE OTHER STUFF YOU WANT TO CAPTURE

DATE: .................................. PLACE: ..................................

## HOW I FELT TODAY:

## WHAT I'VE SEEN TODAY:

_____
_____
_____
_____
_____
_____
_____
_____
_____
_____
_____
_____

## WHAT I ATE TODAY:

_____
_____
_____
_____

## HOW DID WE TRAVEL:

## THE BEST THING THAT HAPPENED TOODAY:

_____
_____

## THE WEATHER TODAY WAS:

PLACE FOR DRAWINGS, PAINTINGS, WRITING, ENTRY TICKETS, PICTURES OR ALL THE OTHER STUFF YOU WANT TO CAPTURE

**DATE:** _____ **PLACE:** _____

**HOW I FELT TODAY:**

| **WHAT I'VE SEEN TODAY:** | **WHAT I ATE TODAY:** |
|---|---|
| _____ | _____ |
| _____ | _____ |
| _____ | _____ |
| _____ | _____ |
| _____ | _____ |
| _____ | **HOW DID WE TRAVEL:** |
| _____ | |
| _____ | |
| _____ | |
| _____ | |
| _____ | |

**THE BEST THING THAT HAPPENED TOODAY:**
_____
_____

**THE WEATHER TODAY WAS:**

PLACE FOR DRAWINGS, PAINTINGS, WRITING, ENTRY TICKETS, PICTURES OR ALL THE OTHER STUFF YOU WANT TO CAPTURE

DATE: _____   PLACE: _____

## HOW I FELT TODAY:

## WHAT I'VE SEEN TODAY:

_____
_____
_____
_____
_____
_____
_____
_____
_____
_____
_____

## WHAT I ATE TODAY:

_____
_____
_____
_____

### HOW DID WE TRAVEL:

## THE BEST THING THAT HAPPENED TOODAY:

_____
_____

## THE WEATHER TODAY WAS:

PLACE FOR DRAWINGS, PAINTINGS, WRITING, ENTRY TICKETS, PICTURES OR ALL THE OTHER STUFF YOU WANT TO CAPTURE

DATE: _____  PLACE: _____

HOW I FELT TODAY:

WHAT I'VE SEEN TODAY:

_____
_____
_____
_____
_____
_____
_____
_____
_____
_____
_____
_____
_____

WHAT I ATE TODAY:

_____
_____
_____
_____
_____

HOW DID WE TRAVEL:

THE BEST THING THAT HAPPENED TOODAY:

_____
_____

THE WEATHER TODAY WAS:

PLACE FOR DRAWINGS, PAINTINGS, WRITING, ENTRY TICKETS, PICTURES OR ALL THE OTHER STUFF YOU WANT TO CAPTURE

Date:                 Place:

How I felt Today:

What I've Seen today:

_____
_____
_____
_____
_____

_____
_____
_____
_____
_____

What I Ate Today:

_____
_____
_____
_____

How did we Travel:

The Best Thing that happened tooday:

_____
_____

The Weather today was:

PLACE FOR DRAWINGS, PAINTINGS, WRITING, ENTRY TICKETS, PICTURES OR ALL THE OTHER STUFF YOU WANT TO CAPTURE

DATE: _____  PLACE: _____

## HOW I FELT TODAY:

## WHAT I'VE SEEN TODAY:

_____
_____
_____
_____
_____
_____
_____
_____
_____
_____
_____
_____

## WHAT I ATE TODAY:

_____
_____
_____
_____

## HOW DID WE TRAVEL:

## THE BEST THING THAT HAPPENED TOODAY:

_____
_____

## THE WEATHER TODAY WAS:

PLACE FOR DRAWINGS, PAINTINGS, WRITING, ENTRY TICKETS, PICTURES OR ALL THE OTHER STUFF YOU WANT TO CAPTURE

DATE: _____  PLACE: _____

## HOW I FELT TODAY:

| WHAT I'VE SEEN TODAY: | WHAT I ATE TODAY: |
|---|---|
| _____ | _____ |
| _____ | _____ |
| _____ | _____ |
| _____ | _____ |
| _____ | _____ |
| _____ | HOW DID WE TRAVEL: |
| _____ | |
| _____ | |
| _____ | |
| _____ | |
| _____ | |

## THE BEST THING THAT HAPPENED TOODAY:
_____
_____

## THE WEATHER TODAY WAS:

PLACE FOR DRAWINGS, PAINTINGS, WRITING, ENTRY TICKETS, PICTURES OR ALL THE OTHER STUFF YOU WANT TO CAPTURE

DATE: _____ | PLACE: _____

## HOW I FELT TODAY:

## WHAT I'VE SEEN TODAY:

_____
_____
_____
_____
_____
_____
_____
_____
_____
_____
_____

## WHAT I ATE TODAY:

_____
_____
_____
_____
_____

### HOW DID WE TRAVEL:

## THE BEST THING THAT HAPPENED TOODAY:

_____
_____

## THE WEATHER TODAY WAS:

PLACE FOR DRAWINGS, PAINTINGS, WRITING, ENTRY TICKETS, PICTURES OR ALL THE OTHER STUFF YOU WANT TO CAPTURE

DATE: ........................................ PLACE: ........................................

HOW I FELT TODAY:

WHAT I'VE SEEN TODAY:

_____
_____
_____
_____
_____
_____
_____
_____
_____
_____
_____
_____

WHAT I ATE TODAY:

_____
_____
_____
_____
_____

HOW DID WE TRAVEL:

THE BEST THING THAT HAPPENED TOODAY:
_____
_____

THE WEATHER TODAY WAS:

PLACE FOR DRAWINGS, PAINTINGS, WRITING, ENTRY TICKETS, PICTURES OR ALL THE OTHER STUFF YOU WANT TO CAPTURE

DATE: _____  PLACE: _____

HOW I FELT TODAY:

WHAT I'VE SEEN TODAY:

_____
_____
_____
_____
_____
_____
_____
_____
_____
_____
_____

WHAT I ATE TODAY:

_____
_____
_____
_____

HOW DID WE TRAVEL:

THE BEST THING THAT HAPPENED TOODAY:
_____
_____

THE WEATHER TODAY WAS:

PLACE FOR DRAWINGS, PAINTINGS, WRITING, ENTRY TICKETS, PICTURES OR ALL THE OTHER STUFF YOU WANT TO CAPTURE

Date: _____ Place: _____

How I felt Today:

How I felt Today:

What I've Seen today:

_____
_____
_____
_____
_____
_____
_____
_____
_____
_____

What I Ate Today:

_____
_____
_____
_____
_____

How did we Travel:

The Best Thing that happened tooday:

_____
_____

The Weather today was:

PLACE FOR DRAWINGS, PAINTINGS, WRITING, ENTRY TICKETS, PICTURES OR ALL THE OTHER STUFF YOU WANT TO CAPTURE

DATE: ................................ PLACE: ................................

HOW I FELT TODAY:

WHAT I'VE SEEN TODAY: | WHAT I ATE TODAY:
_____ | _____
_____ | _____
_____ | _____
_____ | _____
_____ | _____
_____ |
_____ | HOW DID WE TRAVEL:
_____ |
_____ |
_____ |
_____ |

THE BEST THING THAT HAPPENED TOODAY:
_____
_____

THE WEATHER TODAY WAS:

PLACE FOR DRAWINGS, PAINTINGS, WRITING, ENTRY TICKETS, PICTURES OR ALL THE OTHER STUFF YOU WANT TO CAPTURE

Date: ........................... Place: ...........................

How I felt Today:

What I've Seen today:

_____
_____
_____
_____
_____
_____
_____
_____
_____
_____
_____
_____

What I Ate Today:

_____
_____
_____
_____
_____

How did we Travel:

The Best Thing that happened tooday:
_____
_____

The Weather today was:

PLACE FOR DRAWINGS, PAINTINGS, WRITING, ENTRY TICKETS, PICTURES OR ALL THE OTHER STUFF YOU WANT TO CAPTURE

**Date:**          **Place:**

## How I felt Today:

## What I've Seen today:

_____
_____
_____
_____
_____
_____
_____
_____
_____
_____

## What I Ate Today:

_____
_____
_____
_____

### How did we Travel:

## The Best Thing that happened tooday:

_____
_____

## The Weather today was:

PLACE FOR DRAWINGS, PAINTINGS, WRITING, ENTRY TICKETS, PICTURES OR ALL THE OTHER STUFF YOU WANT TO CAPTURE

Date: _____ Place: _____

How I felt Today:

| What I've Seen today: | What I Ate Today: |
|---|---|
| _____ | _____ |
| _____ | _____ |
| _____ | _____ |
| _____ | _____ |
| _____ | _____ |
| _____ | **How did we Travel:** |
| _____ | |
| _____ | |
| _____ | |
| _____ | |
| _____ | |

The Best Thing that happened tooday:
_____
_____

The Weather today was:

PLACE FOR DRAWINGS, PAINTINGS, WRITING, ENTRY TICKETS, PICTURES OR ALL THE OTHER STUFF YOU WANT TO CAPTURE

Date:                  Place:

## How I felt Today:

| What I've Seen today: | What I Ate Today: |
|---|---|
| _____ | _____ |
| _____ | _____ |
| _____ | _____ |
| _____ | _____ |
| _____ | _____ |
| _____ | **How did we Travel:** |
| _____ | |
| _____ | |
| _____ | |
| _____ | |
| _____ | |

## The Best Thing that happened tooday:
_____
_____

## The Weather today was:

PLACE FOR DRAWINGS, PAINTINGS, WRITING, ENTRY TICKETS, PICTURES OR ALL THE OTHER STUFF YOU WANT TO CAPTURE

DATE:                           PLACE:

## HOW I FELT TODAY:

## WHAT I'VE SEEN TODAY:

_____
_____
_____
_____
_____
_____
_____
_____
_____
_____
_____

## WHAT I ATE TODAY:

_____
_____
_____
_____

## HOW DID WE TRAVEL:

## THE BEST THING THAT HAPPENED TOODAY:

_____
_____

## THE WEATHER TODAY WAS:

PLACE FOR DRAWINGS, PAINTINGS, WRITING, ENTRY TICKETS, PICTURES OR ALL THE OTHER STUFF YOU WANT TO CAPTURE

DATE: _____  PLACE: _____

## HOW I FELT TODAY:

😃 🙂 😐 😍 😎 😥

## WHAT I'VE SEEN TODAY:

_____
_____
_____
_____
_____
_____
_____
_____
_____
_____
_____

## WHAT I ATE TODAY:

_____
_____
_____
_____

## HOW DID WE TRAVEL:

## THE BEST THING THAT HAPPENED TOODAY:
_____
_____

## THE WEATHER TODAY WAS:

PLACE FOR DRAWINGS, PAINTINGS, WRITING, ENTRY TICKETS, PICTURES OR ALL THE OTHER STUFF YOU WANT TO CAPTURE

Date: _____  Place: _____

## How I felt Today:

## What I've Seen today:

_____
_____
_____
_____
_____
_____
_____
_____
_____
_____
_____

## What I Ate Today:

_____
_____
_____
_____
_____

## How did we Travel:

## The Best Thing that happened tooday:

_____
_____

## The Weather today was:

PLACE FOR DRAWINGS, PAINTINGS, WRITING, ENTRY TICKETS, PICTURES OR ALL THE OTHER STUFF YOU WANT TO CAPTURE

DATE:        PLACE:

## HOW I FELT TODAY:

## WHAT I'VE SEEN TODAY:

_____
_____
_____
_____
_____
_____
_____
_____
_____
_____
_____

## WHAT I ATE TODAY:

_____
_____
_____
_____
_____

## HOW DID WE TRAVEL:

## THE BEST THING THAT HAPPENED TOODAY:

_____
_____

## THE WEATHER TODAY WAS:

PLACE FOR DRAWINGS, PAINTINGS, WRITING, ENTRY TICKETS, PICTURES OR ALL THE OTHER STUFF YOU WANT TO CAPTURE

Date: _____    Place: _____

## How I felt Today:

| What I've Seen today: | What I Ate Today: |
|---|---|
| _____ | _____ |
| _____ | _____ |
| _____ | _____ |
| _____ | _____ |
| _____ | _____ |
| _____ | **How did we Travel:** |
| _____ | |
| _____ | |
| _____ | |
| _____ | |

## The Best Thing that happened tooday:

_____

_____

## The Weather today was:

PLACE FOR DRAWINGS, PAINTINGS, WRITING, ENTRY TICKETS, PICTURES OR ALL THE OTHER STUFF YOU WANT TO CAPTURE

DATE: _____   PLACE: _____

HOW I FELT TODAY:

WHAT I'VE SEEN TODAY:

_____
_____
_____
_____
_____
_____
_____
_____
_____
_____
_____
_____

WHAT I ATE TODAY:

_____
_____
_____
_____

HOW DID WE TRAVEL:

THE BEST THING THAT HAPPENED TOODAY:
_____
_____

THE WEATHER TODAY WAS:

PLACE FOR DRAWINGS, PAINTINGS, WRITING, ENTRY TICKETS, PICTURES OR ALL THE OTHER STUFF YOU WANT TO CAPTURE

Date: _____  Place: _____

How I felt Today:

| What I've Seen today: | What I Ate Today: |
|---|---|
| _____ | _____ |
| _____ | _____ |
| _____ | _____ |
| _____ | _____ |
| _____ | |
| _____ | How did we Travel: |
| _____ | |
| _____ | |
| _____ | |
| _____ | |

The Best Thing that happened tooday:
_____
_____

The Weather today was:

PLACE FOR DRAWINGS, PAINTINGS, WRITING, ENTRY TICKETS, PICTURES OR ALL THE OTHER STUFF YOU WANT TO CAPTURE

Date:            Place:

## How I felt Today:

## What I've Seen today:

_____

_____

_____

_____

_____

_____

_____

_____

_____

_____

_____

## What I Ate Today:

_____

_____

_____

_____

## How did we Travel:

## The Best Thing that happened tooday:

_____

_____

## The Weather today was:

PLACE FOR DRAWINGS, PAINTINGS, WRITING, ENTRY TICKETS, PICTURES OR ALL THE OTHER STUFF YOU WANT TO CAPTURE

DATE:             PLACE:

## HOW I FELT TODAY:

| WHAT I'VE SEEN TODAY: | WHAT I ATE TODAY: |
|---|---|
| _____ | _____ |
| _____ | _____ |
| _____ | _____ |
| _____ | _____ |
| _____ | _____ |
| _____ | HOW DID WE TRAVEL: |
| _____ | |
| _____ | |
| _____ | |
| _____ | |
| _____ | |

## THE BEST THING THAT HAPPENED TOODAY:
_____
_____

## THE WEATHER TODAY WAS:

PLACE FOR DRAWINGS, PAINTINGS, WRITING, ENTRY TICKETS, PICTURES OR ALL THE OTHER STUFF YOU WANT TO CAPTURE

Date: _____ Place: _____

How I felt Today:

What I've Seen today:

_____
_____
_____
_____
_____
_____
_____
_____
_____
_____

What I Ate Today:

_____
_____
_____
_____

How did we Travel:

The Best Thing that happened tooday:

_____
_____

The Weather today was:

PLACE FOR DRAWINGS, PAINTINGS, WRITING, ENTRY TICKETS, PICTURES OR ALL THE OTHER STUFF YOU WANT TO CAPTURE

DATE: _____     PLACE: _____

HOW I FELT TODAY:

😃 🙂 😐 😍 😎 😣

WHAT I'VE SEEN TODAY:

_____
_____
_____
_____
_____
_____
_____
_____
_____
_____
_____
_____

WHAT I ATE TODAY:

_____
_____
_____
_____
_____

HOW DID WE TRAVEL:

🚂 ✈️ 🚗 🚢

THE BEST THING THAT HAPPENED TOODAY:

_____
_____

THE WEATHER TODAY WAS:

☀️ ☁️ ⛈️ 🌧️ 🌨️

PLACE FOR DRAWINGS, PAINTINGS, WRITING, ENTRY TICKETS, PICTURES OR ALL THE OTHER STUFF YOU WANT TO CAPTURE

Date: _____   Place: _____

## How I felt Today:

| What I've Seen today: | What I Ate Today: |
|---|---|
| _____ | _____ |
| _____ | _____ |
| _____ | _____ |
| _____ | _____ |
| _____ | How did we Travel: |
| _____ | |
| _____ | |
| _____ | |
| _____ | |

The Best Thing that happened tooday:
_____
_____

## THe Weather today was:

PLACE FOR DRAWINGS, PAINTINGS, WRITING, ENTRY TICKETS, PICTURES OR ALL THE OTHER STUFF YOU WANT TO CAPTURE

DATE: _____    PLACE: _____

HOW I FELT TODAY:

WHAT I'VE SEEN TODAY:

_____
_____
_____
_____
_____
_____
_____
_____
_____
_____

WHAT I ATE TODAY:

_____
_____
_____
_____

HOW DID WE TRAVEL:

THE BEST THING THAT HAPPENED TOODAY:

_____
_____

THE WEATHER TODAY WAS:

PLACE FOR DRAWINGS, PAINTINGS, WRITING, ENTRY TICKETS, PICTURES OR ALL THE OTHER STUFF YOU WANT TO CAPTURE

Date: _____ Place: _____

How I felt Today:

| What I've Seen today: | What I Ate Today: |
|---|---|
| _____ | _____ |
| _____ | _____ |
| _____ | _____ |
| _____ | _____ |
| _____ | _____ |
| _____ | How did we Travel: |
| _____ | |
| _____ | |
| _____ | |
| _____ | |

The Best Thing that happened tooday:
_____
_____

The Weather today was:

PLACE FOR DRAWINGS, PAINTINGS, WRITING, ENTRY TICKETS, PICTURES OR ALL THE OTHER STUFF YOU WANT TO CAPTURE

Date: _____   Place: _____

How I felt Today:

| What I've Seen today: | What I Ate Today: |
|---|---|
| _____ | _____ |
| _____ | _____ |
| _____ | _____ |
| _____ | _____ |
| _____ | _____ |
| _____ | |
| _____ | How did we Travel: |
| _____ | |
| _____ | |
| _____ | |
| _____ | |

The Best Thing that happened tooday:
_____
_____

The Weather today was:

PLACE FOR DRAWINGS, PAINTINGS, WRITING, ENTRY TICKETS, PICTURES OR ALL THE OTHER STUFF YOU WANT TO CAPTURE

jonathan kuhla
tempelhofer ufer 15
109 63 berlin
mail: jonathankuhla@gmail.com

Made in United States
North Haven, CT
21 March 2023